RISING

MW00932339

*Embracing Growth and Healing from
Childhood Traumas*

**HARMEL DEANNE CODI, JD, MBA, MDIV
EDITED BY
CYNTHIA L MAXWELL**

PREFACE

As I sit down to pen the preface for "Rising Above: Embracing Growth and Healing from Childhood Traumas," I am acutely aware of the gravity and sensitivity of the subject. This book, while a guide, is also a testament to the resilience of the human spirit. It acknowledges the deep scars that adverse childhood experiences can leave, but more importantly, it is an ode to the possibility of healing and transformation.

The impetus for this book came from the realization that childhood trauma is not a rare, isolated phenomenon but a pervasive part of human experience that crosses all boundaries of geography, culture, and socioeconomic status. It is written for the silent carriers of past pains, for the healers who assist in the recovery process, and for the society that must recognize and address the widespread impacts of these early wounds.

In the following chapters, we explore the manifold ways in which childhood trauma can embed itself into our lives. We look at how it can shape personalities, influence behavior, and even manifest in our physical bodies. However, the heart of this book lies in the transformational power of healing practices. We delve into traditional and contemporary approaches, blending science and spirituality to offer a holistic vision of recovery.

Each chapter is designed to be both a mirror and a window, reflecting personal experiences while offering views from broader perspectives. The real-world examples, stories of resilience, and practical strategies are intended to serve as companions for readers on their own healing journeys.

I have also chosen to include affirmations at the end of each chapter. These are more than mere words; they are intentional phrases crafted to seed hope and foster a sense of agency. They are prompts for the soul, designed to propel the reader forward with a sense of purpose and possibility.

In writing this book, I have drawn not only from the well of professional knowledge and research but also from the deep waters of personal encounters and empathetic connection with those who have experienced childhood trauma. This book is a gift stemming from my training as a hospital chaplain during my tenure in Seminary. I have seen the resilience of the human spirit, and it is this resilience that I hope to nurture in the pages to come.

"Rising Above" is not just a call to heal—it is a recognition of the journey thus far and a guide for the road ahead. It is my heartfelt wish that within these pages, you find understanding, solace, and the keys to unlock a process of healing that is as unique as your story.

By the end of this book, you will have traversed the expansive landscape of childhood traumas and gleaned insights into holistic healing modalities. It is a journey from shadows to light, from pain to healing, from surviving to thriving. Healing Shadows extends a hand to all those affected by childhood traumas, offering understanding, compassion, and hope for a brighter, healed tomorrow.

Welcome to a journey of transformation. Welcome to "Rising Above."

DEDICATION

In humble honor and boundless gratitude to the Creator, who has graciously bestowed upon me the gifts and talents to share with the world.

To my beloved husband, whose unwavering love keeps my heart at peace and whose steadfast support grounds me in every endeavor. I am eternally thankful for your presence in my life.

To my cherished children, you are the beacon of hope that assures me that tomorrow's generations will shine even brighter than the past.

To my extended family, wonderful friends, and dedicated colleagues, your unwavering support sustained my faith in the human experience when the world sought to challenge it.

To all those who have graced my healing retreats and discovered peace, grace, and inner strength, may your journey continue to be illuminated by purpose and transformation.

And to you, dear reader of this book, may the words within its pages lead you to the treasure your heart seeks, and may hope forever guide your desires.

CONTENTS

INTRODUCTION

In the tapestry of our lives, interwoven with moments of joy and celebration, there are also threads of pain, sorrow, and adversity. For many, some of the most profound and lasting of these come from the trials faced during childhood. "Rising Above: Embracing Growth and Healing from Childhood Traumas" is more than just a title; it is a declaration of intent, a beacon of hope, and a map for those who seek to transform their traumas into strength.

Childhood, often painted as a time of innocence and wonder, is also a period of vulnerability. During these formative years, the experiences we undergo shape our worldview, self-worth, and understanding of love and trust. But what happens when these years are punctuated with moments of trauma? How do we move forward when the weight of the past seems too heavy to bear? Can we truly rise above?

This book is designed as a journey. Through its chapters, we'll delve into the deep-rooted impacts of childhood traumas, from the psychological to the physiological and from the spiritual to the societal. But rather than merely charting the shadows, we'll also shine a light on pathways to healing. By embracing holistic perspectives and integrative modalities, we aim to offer not just understanding but also tools and strategies to reclaim one's life and essence.

Every chapter, infused with stories, insights, and affirmations, is a stepping stone on this journey. As you read, may you find solace in knowing you are not alone, strength in the collective wisdom of those who have walked this path before, and inspiration to rise above, embracing growth and healing every step of the way.

Welcome to "Rising Above." Your journey towards healing and transformation begins here.

CHAPTER 1
SILENT ECHOES

Childhood, often painted in strokes of innocence and joy, can also harbor shadows, echoes of experiences that reverberate throughout a lifetime. These silent echoes, manifestations of childhood traumas, range from episodes of abuse to profound losses, each leaving its unique imprint on the soul.

The Many Faces of Trauma

Childhood trauma is not a singular entity; rather, it is a mosaic composed of varied and complex experiences, each piece reflecting a different shade of pain and struggle. Physical abuse, emotional neglect, the sudden loss of a loved one, witnessing domestic violence—these are but a few fragments of the larger picture of childhood trauma (1). The prevalence of such traumas is alarmingly high, with millions of children around the world suffering in silence, their traumas casting long shadows over their lives.

Consider the story of Jane, a bright young girl with sparkling eyes and a radiant smile, yet beneath that joyful façade lingered shadows of emotional neglect and abuse. The constant discord and violence within her family left scars on her soul, transforming her radiant smile into a mask concealing her inner turmoil. Jane's story is, unfortunately, not unique but echoes the silent pain of countless others.

Society's Silent Epidemic

Childhood trauma is often dubbed a silent epidemic, an omnipresent yet overlooked plague that affects a substantial portion of our society. According to a landmark study by Felitti et al. (1998), adverse childhood experiences are major risk factors for the leading causes of illness and death as well as poor quality of life in the United States (1). Children exposed to traumatic events often carry these invisible wounds into adulthood, impacting their mental, emotional, and physical well-being.

This societal epidemic is not isolated to any particular demographic or socioeconomic stratum; it permeates through all layers of society, impacting individuals from varied backgrounds and walks of life (5). It is a collective issue that requires collective acknowledgment, understanding, and action.

The Impact of Loss

Loss is a universal experience, yet for a child, the loss of a loved one can be a profoundly traumatic event, creating ripples that affect their development, relationships, and worldview. Such a loss can become a silent companion, influencing how they view stability, attachment, and love (2). The grief and pain accompanying loss can be

4

overwhelming, creating feelings of abandonment and insecurity that can persist throughout life.

Reflect on the experience of Michael, who lost his mother at the tender age of seven. The world he once knew, filled with warmth and safety, suddenly crumbled, leaving him in a labyrinth of sorrow and confusion. The trauma of this loss became a silent echo in his life, influencing his relationships, his sense of self, and his approach to the world around him.

Navigating the Shadows

To navigate the shadows of childhood trauma is to embark on a journey of understanding and compassion. It involves recognizing the silent echoes of pain and suffering and extending a hand of support and healing to those who bear these invisible scars (4). It requires a holistic approach, one that encompasses the mind, body, and spirit, acknowledging the intricate tapestry of experiences that constitute childhood trauma.

By exploring and understanding the myriad forms of childhood trauma, society can begin to address this silent epidemic, fostering a world where every child can experience the joy and innocence of childhood, free from the shadows of trauma.

Conclusion

Silent Echoes, the resonances of childhood traumas, are prevalent, multifaceted, and deeply impactful, shaping the lives of individuals in myriad ways. From the varied forms of abuse to the profound impacts of loss, each traumatic experience leaves a unique imprint. By acknowledging, understanding, and addressing these silent echoes, society can foster healing and hope, allowing individuals to emerge from the shadows into the light of resilience and renewal.

References

1. Felitti, V. J., Anda, R. F., Nordenberg, D., Williamson, D. F., Spitz, A. M., Edwards, V., ... & Marks, J. S. (1998). Relationship of childhood abuse and household dysfunction to many of the leading causes of death in adults: The Adverse Childhood Experiences (ACE) Study. American journal of preventive medicine, 14(4), 245-252.

2. Perry, B. D., & Szalavitz, M. (2006). *The Boy Who Was Raised as a Dog: And Other Stories from a Child Psychiatrist's Notebook--What Traumatized Children Can Teach Us About Loss, Love, and Healing*. Basic Books.

3. van der Kolk, B. (2014). *The Body Keeps the Score: Brain, Mind, and Body in the Healing of Trauma*. Viking.

4. Levine, P. A. (2010). *In an Unspoken Voice: How the Body Releases Trauma and Restores Goodness*. North Atlantic Books.

5. Herman, J. L. (1997). *Trauma and Recovery: The Aftermath of Violence--from Domestic Abuse to Political Terror*. Basic Books.

Chapter One Affirmations:

1. I embrace the journey of healing from my childhood trauma, recognizing the strength it has fostered within me.

2. Each day, I choose to acknowledge my past with compassion and look toward the future with hope.

3. I accept myself fully, with all my shadows and light, knowing that every part of me deserves love.

4. In the silence of my echoes, I find the voice of my inner peace speaking to me with gentle wisdom.

5. With every breath, I inhale acceptance and exhale judgment, allowing my spirit to rest in tranquility.

6. I am grateful for my resilience and for the lessons my experiences have taught me.

7. I am thankful for the courage to face my past and the strength to shape my future.

8. My journey of healing is my own; I walk this path at my own pace, with grace and self-compassion.

9. I honor the many faces of my trauma as part of my story but not the entirety of my being.

10. In my introspection, I find the power to transform pain into purpose and silence into song.

11. I recognize the epidemic of silence that society harbors, and I choose to be a voice of healing.

12. Each moment of introspection brings me closer to the core of my true spirit, illuminating my path with clarity.

13. There is a light inside of me that never goes out as I move through the shadows.

14. I am not alone in my struggles; shared silence unites us in our quest for peace and understanding.

15. With each step forward, I acknowledge the impact of loss yet embrace the fullness of life that awaits.

16. Gratitude grounds me, providing a foundation of peace amidst the echoes of my past.

17. I celebrate the quiet introspection that brings forth the whispers of my soul's deepest desires for peace.

18. My past may shape me, but it does not define me; I am the architect of my present and future.

19. In the silent echoes of my heart, I find the rhythm of healing that dances to the beat of self-acceptance.

20. I am a beacon of inner peace, shining light on the shadows, transforming them into stepping stones of growth and gratitude.

CHAPTER 2

SHATTERED INNOCENCE

The tendrils of childhood trauma entangle the essence of one's being, reaching into the deepest recesses of the mind, shaping thoughts, behaviors, and the very core of one's psychological development. Shattered innocence delves into the profound impacts of childhood trauma on the psychological fabric of an individual, exploring how such experiences mold cognition and behavior, leaving remnants that can linger a lifetime.

Distorting the Lens of Perception

When children encounter trauma, their developing minds absorb and internalize these experiences, altering their perception of the world and themselves. The once clear lens through which they viewed life becomes clouded, distorting their understanding of safety, trust, and love. These distortions can impact their cognitive development, skewing their ability to process information, solve problems, and make decisions.

Sarah, a vivacious young girl, encountered such distortions when the abuse she suffered silently twisted her perceptions of love and safety. The world became a labyrinth of fear and uncertainty, each step shadowed by the dread of unseen threats. Sarah's journey exemplifies the altered cognition that childhood trauma can engender, a silent struggle faced by many.

Behavioral Echoes

The ripple effects of childhood trauma extend into the realm of behavior, shaping the way individuals react to their environment, relate to others, and cope with stress. The echoes of traumatic experiences manifest in behavioral patterns, often characterized by heightened anxiety, aggression, impulsivity, or withdrawal. The invisible scars of trauma influence the choices one makes, the relationships one forms, and the paths one follows.

Take the example of Alex, whose traumatic experiences led him to build impenetrable walls around his heart, his behaviors marked by detachment and isolation. The pain he endured silently whispered in his actions, echoing the shadows of his past.

Impact on Emotional Regulation

The emotional world of a child who has experienced trauma is often a turbulent sea of conflicting feelings, marked by intense emotions and a struggle to regulate them. The ability to understand, express, and manage emotions becomes compromised, leading to emotional dysregulation and heightened vulnerability to stress.

For instance, consider Emily, who, haunted by the ghosts of her traumatic past, experienced intense emotional storms. Her emotions became turbulent waves, crashing against the shores of her soul, leaving her feeling lost in a sea of despair and confusion.

Learning and Academic Development

The impact of trauma seeps into the learning environment, affecting academic development and achievement. The stress and anxiety stemming from traumatic experiences interfere with the ability to concentrate, retain information, and engage in the learning process. The academic journey becomes a mountainous terrain, each step laden with the weight of unseen burdens.

Reflect on James, who, weighed down by the invisible chains of his trauma, found the journey through the world of learning to be a relentless struggle. His trauma shadowed his every step, whispering in the silence between the words he read, lingering in the numbers he tried to comprehend.

The Journey of Healing

Understanding the profound impacts of childhood trauma on psychological development, cognition, and behavior is a stepping stone on the path to healing. By acknowledging the shattered innocence and the silent echoes of pain, society can extend a hand of support, compassion, and healing to those who carry the invisible scars of their past.

It is a journey toward rebuilding the broken pieces, towards transforming pain into strength, shadows into light.

Conclusion

The shadows of childhood trauma reach deep, shaping the minds, hearts, and behaviors of those who have walked through its silent corridors. Shattered innocence is a journey into understanding these shadows, exploring the ways in which trauma molds psychological development, cognition, and behavior. By peeling back the layers of pain by shining a light on the silent echoes of trauma, we can foster healing, resilience, and hope.

References

1. Perry, B.D., & Szalavitz, M. (2006). *The Boy Who Was Raised as a Dog: And Other Stories from a Child Psychiatrist's Notebook -- What Traumatized Children Can Teach Us About Loss, Love, and Healing.* Basic Books.

2. van der Kolk, B. (2014). *The Body Keeps the Score: Brain, Mind, and Body in the Healing of Trauma.* Viking.

3. Siegel, D.J. (1999). *The Developing Mind: How Relationships and the Brain Interact to Shape Who We Are.* Guilford Press.

4. Levine, P.A., & Kline, M. (2007). *Trauma Through a Child's Eyes: Awakening the Ordinary Miracle of Healing*. North Atlantic Books.

5. Schore, A.N. (2003). *Affect Regulation and the Repair of the Self*. W.W. Norton & Company.

6. Webb, N. B. (Ed.). (2011). *Helping Bereaved Children: A Handbook for Practitioners*. Guilford Press.

Chapter Two Affirmations:

1. I recognize my shattered innocence as a chapter in my story, and I move forward with healing grace.

2. My perceptions are mine to shape; I choose to see the world through a lens of clarity and understanding.

3. I gently guide my behaviors toward positive echoes, creating ripples of healing in my life.

4. With each heartbeat, I learn to regulate my emotions, embracing calmness and inner peace.

5. I am grateful for my ability to feel deeply, for it is a sign of my enduring spirit and capacity for healing.

6. My journey to healing is paved with self-acceptance, as I acknowledge my past without letting it hold me captive.

7. I am patient with my progress, knowing that true growth occurs with time and self-compassion.

8. Every challenge in emotional regulation is an opportunity to learn more about my inner world and to cultivate serenity.

9. I am thankful for my mind's ability to learn and adapt, which aids my academic and personal development.

10. I release the distortions of my past perceptions, allowing my true self to emerge with strength and resilience.

11. The echoes of past behaviors do not control me; I am the master of my actions and my peace.

12. As I grow in my healing, I find gratitude for every step, recognizing my journey as a testament to my perseverance.

13. My emotional regulation is a skill I nurture with care, knowing it leads to a balanced and peaceful heart.

14. In the classroom of life, I am both a dedicated student and a compassionate teacher to myself.

15. The innocence I carry within is not broken but is evolving, becoming wiser and more profound.

16. My healing journey is a path I walk with courage, open to learning and embracing all aspects of myself.

17. I affirm that my past experiences have equipped me with a unique wisdom that enhances my learning and understanding.

18. With gratitude, I acknowledge my progress, knowing that every effort contributes to my healing and academic success.

19. My commitment to introspection helps me untangle complex emotions, leading to a more regulated and harmonious existence.

20. Each day, I choose to step forward on my healing journey with a heart full of gratitude and a spirit ready for renewal.

CHAPTER 3

BEHIND CLOSED DOORS

Behind closed doors, a clandestine theater of pain and fear unfolds, the silent witnesses — children, observing the storm of domestic violence. It is essential to unveil the shrouded impacts that such environments imprint on young minds, altering their perceptions, emotions, and behaviors long into adulthood.

The Invisible Witnesses

Children, the silent observers of domestic violence, absorb the tension, the aggression, the fear permeating their homes. They may not bear the physical scars, but the psychological wounds run deep, echoing throughout their lives. The sight and sound of violence, the volatile ambiance, become the shadows trailing their steps, shaping their worldview, relationships, and very beings.

Take, for example, Lisa, who grew up with the constant clash of anger and despair reverberating through the walls of her home. She became a quiet, introspective soul, the echoes of her childhood painting her life with strokes of anxiety, distrust, and pain.

Shadows on the Psyche

Witnessing domestic violence distorts a child's sense of safety and normalcy. The supposed sanctuaries — home and family — morph into battlegrounds, places where love is overshadowed by fear. This distortion is the seed of psychological struggles, sprouting issues like anxiety, depression, and post-traumatic stress disorder, shadowing the hearts and minds of those who've seen too much too soon.

David, whose earliest memories are marred by the violent dances of his parents, grew up with a shattered sense of security, his mind a battlefield of shadows and fears, a testament to the psychological warfare children undergo in such turbulent environments.

A Pathway to Maladaptive Behaviors

Children raised in the shadows of domestic violence often develop maladaptive coping mechanisms and behavioral patterns. The aggression witnessed becomes a learned response, a tool for navigating a world perceived as hostile. The silent pain translates into actions; the unvoiced screams manifest in the relationships formed and the paths chosen.

Consider Maria, who carried the silent rage of her turbulent childhood into adulthood, her behaviors and choices echoing the chaos of her past. The quiet storm within her was the compass guiding her journey, leading her through the twisted alleys of life.

The Echoes in Relationships

The relationships of those who've grown up witnessing domestic violence are often haunted by the ghosts of their past. The dynamics observed become the blueprint for future relationships—the silent echoes of violence whispering in the bonds formed, the love given and received. The intertwining of love and pain becomes the norm, impacting the ability to form healthy, nurturing relationships.

Reflecting on John, who saw love and violence as two sides of the same coin, his relationships are a reflection of the tumultuous sea he navigated as a child. His bonds were the echoes of his past; the silent whispers of pain and love intermingled.

The Journey Beyond the Shadows

Unveiling the impacts of domestic violence on the silent witnesses is a step toward healing and transformation. By acknowledging the shadows, by understanding the silent echoes, by extending compassion and support, the invisible wounds can begin to heal. It's a journey from the shadows into the light, a pathway to breaking the cycle to transforming pain into strength and fear into hope.

Conclusion

Behind closed doors, the silent witnesses bear the invisible scars of domestic violence, scars that shape their lives in profound ways. The psychological shadows, the maladaptive behaviors, and the echoes in relationships are the remnants of the storms witnessed. By acknowledging and addressing these silent echoes, by extending a hand of compassion and support, we can help in navigating the journey beyond the shadows toward a life marked by resilience, healing, and hope.

References

1. Lundy Bancroft - "Why Does He Do That? Inside the Minds of Angry and Controlling Men" (Berkley Books, 2002).

2. Bessel van der Kolk - "The Body Keeps the Score: Brain, Mind, and Body in the Healing of Trauma" (Penguin Books, 2014).

3. Judith Herman - "Trauma and Recovery: The Aftermath of Violence—From Domestic Abuse to Political Terror" (Basic Books, 1992).

4. Louise Silvern & Carl Auerbach - "Invisible Wounds: A Self-Help Guide for Women in Destructive Relationships" (Hunter House Inc. Publishers, 1986).

5. Susan Forward & Craig Buck - "Toxic Parents: Overcoming Their Hurtful Legacy and Reclaiming Your Life" (Bantam, 2002).

Chapter Three Affirmations:

1. Behind closed doors, I found strength in silence; now, I step into the light with healing courage.

2. I accept the invisible witness that I was, and I honor their journey toward visibility and voice.

3. The shadows that once darkened my psyche now become lessons that teach me self-awareness and growth.

4. I am not my past; I am a survivor, reshaping maladaptive behaviors into stepping stones for success.

5. Gratitude fills me for every moment of introspection that brightens the shadows within my soul.

6. The echoes of past relationships will not dictate my future; I am learning a new language of love and respect.

7. I breathe in peace and exhale turmoil, allowing inner calm to permeate the once-closed spaces of my heart.

8. With self-acceptance, I acknowledge my journey, understanding that even behind closed doors, my spirit was growing.

9. Every step I take is a movement away from the shadows, into a life that I choose and shape with intention.

10. I am the architect of my relationships; I build them on foundations of trust, healing, and mutual respect.

11. I cherish the ability to look within, to shine a light on the shadows, and to embrace the truths discovered there.

12. My journey beyond the shadows is paved with lessons of resilience and the promise of new beginnings.

13. Each day, I am thankful for the strength I find in the once-invisible parts of me that now stand bold and bright.

14. As I heal, I transform the echoes of my relationships into harmonious melodies of connection and self-respect.

15. Inner peace is my sanctuary, and with each introspective thought, I fortify the walls with compassion and understanding.

16. I release the shadows cast by others and illuminate my path with my own light, strong and unwavering.

17. The pathway that once led to maladaptive behaviors now guides me to choices that align with my well-being.

18. I honor my past as the invisible witness, and now I step forward as a visible testament to healing and hope.

19. Gratitude guides me to recognize the intricate patterns of my psyche, weaving them into a tapestry of insightful introspection.

20. Beyond the shadows, there is a horizon bright with possibility, and I journey towards it with a heart full of peace and a spirit unbound.

CHAPTER 4

BULLIED SOULS

In the realm of childhood sorrows, the silent cry of bullied souls resonates, echoing the pain of ridicule, exclusion, and torment. Bullying, a malignant shadow in the lives of many, comes in varied forms, each leaving its imprint on mental health and self-esteem. This chapter aims to unfold the layers of pain embedded in bullied souls, seeking to understand and heal the wounds etched by the sharp claws of oppression.

The Many Faces of Bullying

Bullying wears many faces, from the blatant aggression of physical torment to the subtle sting of verbal ridicule and the invisible wounds of cyberbullying. Whether it is the mocking laughter, the derisive words, or the isolating whispers, each form of bullying cuts deep, engraving scars on the psyche (1).

Remember Jamie, a child whose days were clouded by the constant rain of mocking words and isolating whispers. His world became a maze of shadows, each corner whispering the silent echoes of ridicule, each step weighed down by the chains of exclusion.

The Echoes of Pain

The pain of being bullied reverberates long after the visible wounds have healed, shaping thoughts, emotions, and self-perception. The whispers of worthlessness become the soundtrack of bullied souls, the silent screams of pain shadowing their every step. The heartache of being singled out, of feeling less-than, pierces the essence of one's being, sowing seeds of self-doubt, anxiety, and depression (2).

Consider Emma, whose spirit was crushed under the weight of relentless bullying. The silent echoes of pain became her constant companions, the shadows of worthlessness clouding her vision, whispering in her ears the tales of her insignificance.

The Impact on Self-Esteem

Bullying, with its relentless assault on the psyche, erodes self-esteem, leaving behind a shattered reflection of one's worth. The incessant messages of inadequacy, of being unwanted and unloved, corrode the foundations of self-belief and self-worth, fostering a distorted self-image (3).

Reflect on Michael, whose self-esteem was a fragile construct, broken and rebuilt over and over again by the endless cycle of bullying. His reflection in the mirror was a distorted echo of the ridicule and exclusion he endured, a silent reminder of his perceived unworthiness.

The Mental Health Struggle

The invisible wounds of bullying manifest in the mental health struggles of those who bear them. The silent pain translates into anxiety, depression, and a myriad of other psychological challenges, the echoes of ridicule and exclusion a constant undercurrent in their minds (4). The battle with one's demons becomes a daily ordeal, a silent struggle overshadowed by the laughter and whispers of the past.

Look at Sophia, who, despite the smiles she painted on her face, battled the demons of her past every day. Her laughter was the mask she wore to hide the silent tears; her brightness was a façade to conceal the shadows within.

Moving Beyond the Pain

Understanding the pain of bullied souls is a gateway to healing and transformation. By acknowledging the many faces of bullying, by extending a hand of compassion and support, and by empowering the silenced voices, we can begin to mend the broken spirits, rebuild the shattered self-esteem, and erase the echoes of pain (5).

Conclusion

Bullied souls bear the invisible scars of ridicule, exclusion, and torment, the echoes of pain shadowing their lives. The many faces of bullying engrave deep wounds on mental health and self-esteem, whispering silent tales of worthlessness and despair. By unveiling the shadows, by understanding the pain, by extending compassion and support, we can help in navigating the journey beyond the shadows toward a life marked by resilience, healing, and hope.

References

1. Olweus, D. (1993). *Bullying at School: What We Know and What We Can Do*. Blackwell.

2. Coloroso, B. (2003). *The Bully, the Bullied, and the Bystander: From Preschool to High School, How Parents and Teachers Can Help Break the Cycle of Violence*. HarperResource.

3. Rigby, K. (2002). *New Perspectives on Bullying*. Jessica Kingsley Publishers.

4. Garbarino, J., & deLara, E. W. (2002). *And Words Can Hurt Forever: How to Protect Adolescents from Bullying, Harassment, and Emotional Violence*. Free Press.

5. Wiseman, R. (2002). *Queen Bees and Wannabes: Helping Your Daughter Survive Cliques, Gossip, Boyfriends, and Other Realities of Adolescence*. Crown.

Chapter Four Affirmations:

1. I am more than the many faces of bullying; I am a mosaic of strength, courage, and resilience.

2. With every echo of past pain, I choose to respond with a whisper of compassion for myself.

3. My self-esteem is a garden I tend to with care; no footstep of bullying can trample its growth anymore.

4. I embrace the mental struggles as signs of my inner battles, knowing each victory leads to greater peace.

5. In healing from childhood trauma, I find a deep well of inner peace that no harsh word can disturb.

6. I give thanks for my journey, for in the struggle, I have discovered my undeniable power and worth.

7. The echoes of pain are fading into the past, replaced by the clear tones of self-acceptance and love.

8. I choose to see the impact on my self-esteem not as a scar, but as a badge of my triumph and resilience.

9. Each day, I step further away from the shadows of bullying, into the sunlight of my own validation.

10. My mental struggles have become my strengths, each one a stepping stone on the path to healing.

11. With gratitude, I honor every experience that has led me to this point of introspection and growth.

12. I am reclaiming my narrative, moving beyond the pain, writing chapters of joy and self-fulfillment.

13. My soul whispers affirmations of self-love and acceptance, drowning out the noise of past bullies.

14. In the face of bullying's many masks, I stand firm in the truth of my own beautiful identity.

15. Each tear shed has watered the soil of my self-esteem, from which now blooms a confident and peaceful spirit.

16. I acknowledge my mental struggle but also celebrate the clarity and understanding that comes with healing.

17. The bullying I endured will not define my future; I am moving forward with a heart full of grace and dignity.

18. I honor my inner child, soothing the echoes of pain with gentle words of courage and self-compassion.

19. With each step beyond the pain, I cultivate a spirit of gratitude for the strength I've gained and the peace I've found.

20. My journey of healing has taught me the power of self-acceptance, turning bullied souls into beacons of hope and transformation.

CHAPTER 5

THE CHAIN OF LOSS

The chain of loss, with its links of pain and absence, wraps around the hearts of those who have experienced the anguish of losing a loved one. Bereavement leaves a profound impact on the human spirit, particularly on children who lose their parents or guardians. This chapter seeks to delve deeper into understanding how such loss affects the emotional and developmental realms of children, hoping to shed light on the silent sorrow that encompasses their being.

The Burden of Absence

When a child loses a parent or guardian, they are thrust into a world shrouded in absence and longing. The void left behind becomes a silent companion, a constant reminder of what once was (1). The routine comfort—the everyday assurances, the whispers of love and safety—vanished, leaving in their wake a world unmoored and aching.

Think of Lucy, a vibrant soul who suddenly plunged into a world without the guiding light of her mother. The vacuum created by her absence was a silent agony, a constant echo of lost love and unspoken words.

Emotional Turmoil

Children who have lost a parent or sibling go through an emotional storm in silence, with waves of sadness, rage, and confusion crashing against the shores of their hearts (5). The journey through the landscapes of sorrow is fraught with unshed tears, unvoiced screams, and unanswered questions (2). The emotional upheaval can disrupt their developmental journey, altering their perception of the world and themselves.

For instance, William, who lost his father at a tender age, became a silent wanderer in the world of grief, his heart a battlefield of unspoken pain and unshed tears. The emotional turmoil within him was a constant companion, whispering tales of loss and longing.

Impacts on Development

The loss of a parent or guardian interrupts the developmental journey of children. The security and stability integral to their growth are replaced by uncertainty and upheaval. The silent sorrow acts as a barrier, influencing their cognitive, social, and emotional development, shaping their interactions, learning, and worldview (3).

Emily, orphaned early in life, grew up with the shadows of loss clouding her developmental path. Her journey was a silent struggle, with the echoes of absence influencing her learning, relationships, and perception of the world.

The Path to Resilience

Understanding the pain of loss and its impact on children's development is the first step toward resilience. By acknowledging the silent sorrow, by extending a hand of compassion and support, and by creating environments of understanding and acceptance, we can help in navigating the journey through the landscapes of grief towards healing and growth (4).

Conclusion

The chain of loss leaves a profound imprint on the hearts and development of bereaved children. The burden of absence, the emotional turmoil, and the interrupted developmental journey are the silent echoes of bereavement. By extending compassion, understanding, and support, we can help light the path through the shadows of loss toward resilience, healing, and hope.

References

1. Worden, J. William. "Grief Counseling and Grief Therapy: A Handbook for the Mental Health Practitioner." Springer Publishing Company, 4th Edition.

2. Perry, Bruce D., and Szalavitz, Maia. "The Boy Who Was Raised as a Dog: And Other Stories from a Child Psychiatrist's Notebook." Basic Books.

3. Malchiodi, Cathy A. "Creative Interventions with Traumatized Children." The Guilford Press.

4. Neimeyer, Robert A. "Techniques of Grief Therapy: Creative Practices for Counseling the Bereaved." Routledge.

5. Webb, N. B. (Ed.). (2011). *Helping Bereaved Children: A Handbook for Practitioners*. Guilford Press.

Chapter Five Affirmations:

1. The chain of loss that once held me is transforming into a ladder of growth and self-discovery.

2. I release the burden of absence, filling its space with self-acceptance and the presence of my own love.

3. Through emotional turmoil, I navigate a course to tranquility, embracing the waves as they come and go.

4. Every impact on my development has been a lesson, sculpting me into a more intricate and resilient self.

5. On the path to resilience, I find solace in the inner peace that blooms quietly within me.

6. I am grateful for my ability to turn loss into introspection, finding in my spirit a wellspring of wisdom.

7. With each breath, I strengthen the chain of self-compassion, more potent than any loss I've experienced.

8. The absence I've felt has become a teacher, guiding me towards a reunion with all parts of my being.

9. In my emotional turmoil, I discover the seeds of peace, planting them with intentions of growth and healing.

10. My development, influenced by loss, now propels me forward with a profound sense of purpose and self-awareness.

11. Resilience is my birthright, and I claim it now with every step I take on this healing journey.

12. I give thanks for the strength that has emerged from the burden of absence, illuminating the path ahead.

13. The turmoil that once shook me now serves as the foundation upon which I build my temple of peace.

14. Each challenge in my development has fortified my soul, equipping me with an unshakeable sense of self.

15. I am not alone on this path to resilience; I am accompanied by an inner peace that never falters.

16. Gratitude fills me for the chain of loss has led to a circle of healing, encompassing all that I am.

17. As I accept the intricacies of my journey, the burden of absence lightens, replaced by a liberating self-acceptance.

18. Emotional turmoil has taught me the language of the heart, and now I speak it fluently with love and empathy.

19. I recognize that every impact on my development is an opportunity to learn, grow, and thrive.

20. Walking the path to resilience, I embrace each loss as a stepping stone to a more robust, peaceful, and whole existence.

CHAPTER 6

SCARS OF NEGLECT

When the warmth of presence is replaced by the cold shadows of absence, when the silence of neglect returns the echoes of laughter and love, the scars etched on the soul are deep and enduring. Neglect and abandonment create an invisible tapestry of pain, affecting emotional development and attachment profoundly. This chapter ventures into the silent world of neglected souls, exploring the lasting impacts and the journey toward healing.

The Silent Suffering

Neglect is a silent form of suffering where the absence of care, attention, and affection creates a void, a silent echo of what should have been. It is a world where the comforting embrace is missing, and the reassuring words are unheard, leaving children wandering in the shadows of their unmet needs and unfulfilled longings (1).

Consider the story of Ava, whose world was a silent realm of longing, a space where the echoes of neglect whispered the tales of absence and unlove. Her journey was marked by the unmet gazes, the unheard cries, the untouched hands.

Emotional Development: A Hindered Journey

The silent scars of neglect impact the emotional development of children significantly. The lack of nurturing and emotional availability hinders the formation of healthy emotional responses and regulation (2). The emotional landscape becomes a terrain of instability, where expressing and understanding emotions become arduous tasks and forming emotional connections seems like a distant dream.

For example, imagine Noah, a young boy enveloped in the shadows of neglect, struggling to navigate the intricate tapestry of emotions. His emotional responses were fragments of unlearned lessons, his ability to connect a puzzle of unmet needs.

Impact on Attachment

Neglect creates a ripple effect on the attachment patterns of children. The absence of a secure base of a comforting presence creates an environment of insecurity and instability. The attachment figures, instead of being sources of safety and assurance, become representations of unreliability and unpredictability (3). This affects the ability to form secure and stable relationships, leading to a spectrum of attachment issues in later life.

Reflecting on Mia, who grew up in the echoes of neglect, her attachment figures the shadows of inconsistency and unavailability. Her relationships were a maze of insecurity, a journey through the landscapes of detachment and fear.

Seeking Healing and Connection

Understanding the silent scars of neglect and abandonment is essential in fostering healing and connection. Recognizing the unmet needs, the unfulfilled longings, and the unlearned emotional lessons paves the way for rebuilding the foundations of emotional development and attachment (4). Providing environments of consistency, reliability, and emotional availability can help in mending the broken links of attachment and fostering emotional growth.

Conclusion

Neglect and abandonment leave invisible scars, hindering emotional development and deeply affecting attachment. The silent suffering, the delayed emotional journey, and the insecure attachments are the shadows of neglect. By unveiling the silent scars by fostering understanding, consistency, and emotional availability, we can light the path toward healing, connection, and emotional resilience.

References

1. Perry, B. D., & Szalavitz, M. (2007). *The Boy Who Was Raised as a Dog: And Other Stories from a Child Psychiatrist's Notebook – What Traumatized Children Can Teach Us About Loss, Love, and Healing*. Basic Books.

2. Hughes, D. A. (2006). *Building the Bonds of Attachment: Awakening Love in Deeply Traumatized Children.* Rowman & Littlefield Publishers.

3. van der Kolk, B. (2014). *The Body Keeps the Score: Brain, Mind, and Body in the Healing of Trauma.* Viking.

4. Webb, N. B. (Ed.). (2011). *Working With Traumatized Youth in Child Welfare.* The Guilford Press.

Chapter Six Affirmations:

1. My scars of neglect are not a life sentence; they are my teachers, guiding me towards deep healing and self-compassion.

2. I honor my silent suffering by giving it a voice through my strength and my pursuit of peace.

3. My emotional development continues each day, unhindered by the past, as I embrace growth with open arms.

4. I understand the impact of my attachment wounds, and I choose to relearn connection with kindness and patience.

5. In seeking healing, I am not alone; I am joined by the wisdom of my experiences and the support of the universe.

6. I am more than the neglect I faced; I am a wellspring of potential, love, and boundless peace.

7. With each introspective journey, I uncover layers of my spirit, nurturing them back to health with gentle self-acceptance.

8. The silent suffering within me is met with a louder voice of resilience, self-care, and understanding.

9. I am grateful for my ability to transform hindered emotional development into a path of enlightened emotional maturity.

10. My impact on attachment forms a blueprint for building stronger, more meaningful connections now.

11. As I seek healing and connection, I find solace in the inner peace that was always waiting within.

12. The scars of my past become the roadmaps to compassion for myself and for others.

13. Each day, I choose to soften the scars of neglect with affirmations of self-love and actions of self-care.

14. I am redefining my emotional development, taking the lead in my journey towards wholeness.

15. The impact of past neglect is being undone through present moments of gratitude and the power of my inner spirit.

16. In my quest for connection, I am discovering a universe within me, rich with love and peace.

17. Each step towards healing from neglect is a step towards the unconditional self-acceptance I rightfully deserve.

18. My silent suffering becomes a wellspring of empathy, making me a beacon of comfort to others.

19. The impact on my early attachments paves the way for forming healthier bonds that nourish my soul.

20. Through the neglect, I have grown; through introspection, I heal; with gratitude, I embrace the journey ahead.

CHAPTER 7

THE BODY REMEMBERS

The profound resonance of childhood trauma is not limited to the confines of our minds. It echoes throughout our bodies, leaving traces in our very cells, our brain's pathways, and even the rhythms of our hearts. "The Body Remembers" is a phrase often used in therapeutic circles, and with good reason. Even when traumatic memories fade or are repressed, the body silently holds onto them, translating emotional pain into physical symptoms and patterns. Dive with us into the intricate ways our bodies bear the imprints of traumatic experiences from our youth.

An Imprint on the Brain

The brain, being the core of our perception and response to the world, is highly sensitive to traumatic experiences, especially during formative years. Trauma can affect neural connections and pathways, altering cognition, memory, and even emotional responses.

For instance, research has shown that traumatic experiences in childhood can impact the amygdala, the area of the brain involved in processing emotions and detecting threats (1). It becomes hyper-reactive, often leading to heightened states of anxiety and alertness even in non-threatening situations. Children who faced frequent traumas might develop a brain that is perpetually on guard, constantly expecting danger.

Stress Response: Always on High Alert

A significant physiological change can be observed in the body's stress response system. Traumatic events often trigger a "fight, flight, or freeze" response. When trauma is frequent or chronic, this system can go into overdrive, leading to prolonged periods of cortisol release, the body's main stress hormone (2). Over time, this constant state of alertness can lead to wear and tear on the body, resulting in conditions like chronic fatigue, immune system deficiencies, and even cardiovascular issues.

Imagine the case of Jamie, who experienced recurrent trauma in childhood. As an adult, Jamie would often find himself overreacting to minor stresses, his heart racing, palms sweaty, and mind racing at the slightest hint of confrontation. His body, having grown accustomed to a high-alert state during childhood, continued to respond in the same way, even when the threats of his past no longer existed.

The Heart and the Mind: Inextricable Links

The heart, too, bears the burden of traumatic memories. Research indicates a strong correlation between adverse childhood experiences and cardiovascular issues in adulthood (3). Emotional pain and stress, if chronic, can lead to an array of health problems, from high blood pressure to an increased risk of heart disease.

Manifestations: Physical Symptoms of Hidden Wounds

Sometimes, the body cries out in ways that words cannot express. Unresolved traumas might manifest as chronic pain, migraines, digestive issues, and even autoimmune disorders. These are the body's ways of signaling that something's amiss, a cry for help that the traumatic experience still lingers and seeks resolution.

Healing: Tuning into the Body's Wisdom

Recognizing these physiological responses to trauma is essential, not just for mental well-being but for holistic health. Therapies that bridge the mind-body divide, such as somatic experiencing or trauma-informed yoga, have been shown to be effective in helping individuals reconnect with their bodies, release stored traumas, and pave a path toward healing (4).

Conclusion

The interwoven tapestry of mind and body is delicate, holding onto memories and experiences in intricate patterns. Childhood traumas etch imprints not just on our psyche but also on our physiological being. By understanding this deep connection, we pave the way for holistic healing, ensuring that both the mind and the body find their way back to harmony.

This chapter touches upon the profound connections between traumatic experiences and their physical manifestations. By bridging the understanding of these intricate connections, we can pave a comprehensive path toward healing, taking into account both our emotional and physical well-being.

References

1. Teicher, M. H., Samson, J. A., Anderson, C. M., & Ohashi, K. (2016). *The effects of childhood maltreatment on brain structure, function, and connectivity.* Nature Reviews Neuroscience, 17(10), 652-666.

2. Heim, C., & Nemeroff, C. B. (2001). *The role of childhood trauma in the neurobiology of mood and anxiety disorders: Preclinical and clinical studies.* Biological Psychiatry, 49(12), 1023-1039.

3. Felitti, V. J., Anda, R. F., Nordenberg, D., Williamson, D. F., Spitz, A. M., Edwards, V., ... & Marks, J. S. (1998). *Relationship of childhood abuse and household dysfunction to many of the leading causes of death in adults: The Adverse Childhood Experiences (ACE) Study.* American Journal of Preventive Medicine, 14(4), 245-258.

4. van der Kolk, B. A. (2014). *The Body Keeps the Score: Brain, Mind, and Body in the Healing of Trauma.* Penguin Books.

Chapter Seven Affirmations:

1. My body's memories of trauma are a testament to my resilience and my capacity for healing and renewal.

2. I trust in the wisdom of my body to heal, and I honor its journey through gentle care and mindful attention.

3. As I acknowledge the imprints on my brain, I also celebrate its plasticity and my power to reshape it with positive experiences.

4. Though my stress response was once on high alert, I now breathe deeply, inviting calm and restoring balance.

5. I embrace the link between heart and mind, nurturing both with compassion and understanding as I heal.

6. With each mindful breath, I loosen the hold of hidden wounds, allowing for healing and inner peace.

7. I am grateful for my body's signals, guiding me toward the care and nurturing it needs and deserves.

8. My physical symptoms are not my enemies; they are messengers, and I listen to them with kindness and curiosity.

9. In the sanctuary of introspection, I uncover the strength to transform pain into a path of wellness.

10. Every cell in my body holds the potential for peace, and I tap into this reservoir with gratitude each day.

11. The wisdom of my body is a treasure, and I turn towards it with openness, ready to learn and to heal.

12. As I accept my body's memories, I create new ones filled with joy, strength, and tranquility.

13. I am not defined by my body's past response to trauma; I am molded by my present courage to overcome it.

14. With each heartbeat, I reaffirm my commitment to nurturing the mind-body connection and fostering healing.

15. I give thanks for my body's resilience, an unwavering ally in my journey to wholeness.

16. Turning inward, I embrace the body's wisdom, finding solace in its capacity to recover and flourish.

17. My awareness of the body's memory lights the way for profound healing and the return to inner peace.

18. Physical manifestations of trauma dissolve as I affirm my dedication to self-care and embrace the healing process.

19. My spirit and body converse in a language of healing, and I am the patient and attentive listener.

20. By honoring the body's wisdom, I allow the imprints of the past to transform into the foundations of a healed future.

CHAPTER 8

SHROUDED MIND

Childhood is often painted as a carefree period filled with whimsy, imagination, and play. However, for many, it's also a time when seeds of trauma can be planted seeds that, if left untended, can grow into formidable trees of anxiety, depression, PTSD, and more. Childhood traumas do not just create immediate pain; they can lay dormant, only to re-emerge in various forms in one's adult life. Let's journey into the realm of the shrouded mind to uncover the deep-seated mental repercussions of such traumas.

Anxiety: The Restless Shadow

The whispers of past traumas often manifest as the pervasive echoes of anxiety. This state of heightened alertness is the body and mind's protective mechanism, once valuable for traumatic situations but now acting like an overzealous guard in peaceful times (1).

Consider Emily, who faced significant emotional neglect as a child. As an adult, she often felt overwhelmed in social situations, constantly feeling judged or out of place. These weren't mere "butterflies in the stomach"; they were debilitating thoughts rooted in her childhood experiences that made it hard for her to form close relationships.

Depression: The Heavy Cloak

While anxiety keeps one on edge, depression acts as a heavy, suffocating cloak, pulling one down into the depths of despair. Childhood traumas, especially those involving neglect or abuse, can result in feelings of unworthiness or self-blame that carry into adulthood (2).

Meet Jordan, who experienced physical abuse during his early years. As he grew older, he grappled with recurring phases of deep sadness and a feeling of emptiness. The joyous moments of life felt distant as if observed through a thick, foggy glass. For Jordan, the echoes of the past dimmed the brightness of the present.

PTSD: Reliving the Pain

Post-traumatic stress disorder (PTSD) is perhaps the most direct mental health consequence of trauma. For individuals with PTSD, the traumatic events of the past are not just memories; they are vivid, recurrent nightmares that intrude upon the present (3).

Take the case of Sophia, who witnessed a traumatic event in her childhood. Even decades later, certain sounds, sights, or even smells would catapult her back to that fateful day, making her heart race and her mind spin. Sophia was trapped in a relentless cycle of reliving her trauma, a prisoner of her memories.

A Symphony of Symptoms

It's crucial to realize that these mental health repercussions rarely exist in isolation. They often intertwine, creating a complex web of symptoms. For instance, anxiety could lead to depressive episodes, and those with PTSD could simultaneously grapple with severe anxiety attacks.

Paths to Healing: Acknowledging and Seeking

One of the most potent antidotes to the shadows of childhood trauma is acknowledgment—recognizing the trauma's impact and seeking help. Therapy, counseling, and support groups can offer guidance, providing tools and strategies to navigate and heal from the mental health challenges rooted in childhood experiences (4).

Conclusion

The shadows of past traumas can indeed make the mind appear mysterious. But with understanding, support, and professional guidance, the clouds can part, revealing the radiant potential of healing and growth. Our traumas might shape us, but they don't define us. And in acknowledging their impacts, we take the first step toward a brighter mental landscape.

Through stories and studies, this chapter unveils the profound impacts of childhood trauma on mental well-being. Recognizing these shadows and seeking help can set one on a healing journey, proving that the past might shape us, but the future still holds infinite potential for growth and happiness.

References

1. Pine, D. S. (2003). *Developmental psychobiology and response to threats: relevance to trauma in children and adolescents.* Biological Psychiatry, 53(9), 796-808.

2. Kendler, K. S., Kuhn, J., & Prescott, C. A. (2004). *The interrelationship of neuroticism, sex, and stressful life events in the prediction of episodes of major depression.* American Journal of Psychiatry, 161(4), 631-636.

3. American Psychiatric Association. (2013). *Diagnostic and statistical manual of mental disorders (DSM-5®).* American Psychiatric Pub.

4. van der Kolk, B. A. (2015). *The Body Keeps the Score: Brain, Mind, and Body in the Healing of Trauma.* Penguin Books.

Chapter Eight Affirmations:

1. In the quiet of my mind, I acknowledge the shadows, yet choose to walk towards the light of healing.

2. Each breath is a step away from anxiety's restless shadow and into the calm of present awareness.

3. I shed the heavy cloak of depression, layer by layer, revealing the resilient self beneath, capable of joy.

4. I accept my experience with PTSD as part of my story, but not its entirety, as I seek moments of peace.

5. Harmony arises as I tune the symphony of my symptoms into a melody of self-compassion and hope.

6. I am more than my anxious thoughts; I am a haven of tranquility, and I invite serenity into my mind.

7. With gratitude, I recognize my mind's protective measures and gently guide it back to a state of balance.

8. I wear self-acceptance as armor, shielding myself from the barrage of depression's whispers.

9. As I navigate PTSD's waves, I hold onto the anchor of inner peace, knowing the storm will pass.

10. In the dissonance of mental distress, I seek the notes that resonate with calmness and self-care.

11. My mind's shroud lifts with each act of self-love, revealing a clear vision of my healing journey.

12. Even when anxiety flutters within me, I remain grounded in the knowledge of my inherent worth.

13. I honor my experience with depression but choose to define my horizon with hope and light.

14. Reliving pain becomes a path to wisdom as I transform past trauma into lessons of strength.

15. I am the composer of my mind's symphony, and I choose chords of peace and self-compassion.

16. I thank my mind for its efforts to protect me and guide it towards thoughts of acceptance and recovery.

17. Within me is a sanctuary of calm, untouched by the shadows, where I rest and rejuvenate my spirit.

18. Depression's weight lifts as I affirm my ability to rise, buoyed by the support of my inner spirit.

19. Every flashback, every intrusive thought, is met with the powerful antidote of my mindful presence.

20. My symphony of symptoms merges into a chorus of healing, as I honor the journey and embrace a future of well-being.

CHAPTER 9

HOLISTIC PERSPECTIVES

Imagine, if you will, a beautifully woven tapestry. Each thread contributes to the whole, creating a masterpiece that's much more than the sum of its parts. Our being – our mind, body, and spirit – is much like that tapestry. When one thread is affected, the entire tapestry feels the pull. This is the foundation of the holistic approach: understanding and treating the individual as a complete, interconnected entity. Dive with me into this chapter as we unravel the intricate dance of trauma and healing from a holistic viewpoint.

Understanding Holism

The term "holistic" originates from the Greek word "holos," which means "whole." At its core, holism is about recognizing the interconnectedness of all aspects of an individual's well-being (1). It implies that to heal truly and deeply, one must address not only the mind or body alone but the collective symphony of the mind, body, and spirit.

Mind-Body Connection: More Than Just a Phrase

Science is increasingly shining a light on the deep links between our mental and physical states. For instance, chronic stress, often stemming from traumatic experiences, can lead to physical ailments like heart disease and weakened immune function (2). Conversely, physical pain can lead to mental distress.

Consider Lila, a bright young woman who experienced a traumatic injury in her teens. While the physical wounds healed with time, the emotional scars lingered, manifesting as anxiety and occasional depressive episodes. Her trauma wasn't just in the mind; it echoed throughout her body.

The Spirit: Often Overlooked, But Never Absent

While discussions around trauma often focus on the mind and body, the spirit, or the essence of who we are beyond the physical and mental, plays a silent yet powerful role. Spiritual pain, often manifesting as a loss of purpose or meaning, can be just as debilitating as any physical ailment (3).

Reflect on Raj, who faced significant emotional abuse during childhood. As an adult, while therapy helped him manage anxiety, he often felt adrift—a sense of disconnection from the world around him. It wasn't until he embarked on a spiritual journey, embracing practices like meditation and mindfulness, that he began to find inner peace and purpose.

Healing: The Holistic Dance

True healing, as advocated by holistic practitioners, seeks to balance the mind, body, and spirit. It's not about silencing symptoms but about re-establishing harmony within the entire being.

Yoga, for instance, doesn't just offer physical benefits; it's also a mental exercise, teaching practitioners to stay present and find peace within (4). Similarly, practices like acupuncture or even specific dietary changes can profoundly affect mental well-being.

Embracing the Tapestry

Recognizing the holistic nature of our being can be both empowering and liberating. It suggests that every action we take, every bite of food, every thought, and every breath is a step toward either healing or harm. And, by weaving together practices that nourish the mind, body, and spirit, we can create a tapestry of well-being that's resilient, vibrant, and beautifully whole.

Conclusion

In the realm of trauma and healing, there's no one-size-fits-all. But by embracing the holistic perspective, we acknowledge the intricate interplay of the mind, body, and spirit, paving the way for profound, all-encompassing healing. After all, we're not just a collection of parts; we're a beautifully woven tapestry, deserving of care in its entirety.

This chapter underlines the beauty of holism and its significance in our journey through trauma and healing. By treating ourselves as an interconnected entity, we can find deeper, more resonant paths to healing and wholeness.

References

1. Smuts, J.C. (1926). *Holism and Evolution*. Macmillan.

2. McEwen, B. S. (2004). *Protection and damage from acute and chronic stress: Allostasis and allostatic overload and relevance to the pathophysiology of psychiatric disorders.* Annals of the New York Academy of Sciences, 1032(1), 1-7.

3. Puchalski, C. M., Vitillo, R., Hull, S. K., & Reller, N. (2014). *Improving the spiritual dimension of whole person care: Reaching national and international consensus.* Journal of palliative medicine, 17(6), 642-656.

4. Khalsa, S. B. S., Cohen, L., McCall, T., & Telles, S. (2016). *The principles and practice of yoga in health care.* Handspring Publishing.

Chapter Nine Affirmations:

1. I embrace the holistic nature of healing, recognizing that my well-being weaves together the physical, emotional, and spiritual.

2. In understanding holism, I see myself as a complete universe, where every part of me works in harmony towards healing.

3. The mind-body connection is my foundation for peace; my thoughts soothe my cells, and my cells inform my thoughts.

4. I honor my spirit, an eternal flame that guides me through the healing journey, often quiet but always present.

5. Healing is a dance, and I move to its rhythm, stepping through shadows and light with equal grace and strength.

6. My spirit, mind, and body are a tapestry of resilience; I embrace their unity as I heal from my childhood trauma.

7. With every mindful step, I acknowledge the profound connection between my inner world and my physical experience.

8. I give thanks for the integration of my being, where the spirit's whispers and the body's signals meet and are understood.

9. In the holistic dance of healing, I am both the dancer and the music, creating a harmony that resonates with self-acceptance and peace.

10. As I journey inward, I uncover the powerful alliance between every aspect of my self, drawing on this strength for healing.

11. I am grateful for the holistic perspective that allows me to see the full picture of my healing, a mosaic made whole with love and care.

12. My spirit is an integral part of my healing, a beacon that shines on the paths of inner peace and self-discovery.

13. I affirm that the spirit's role in healing is undeniable, providing depth and dimension to my journey toward wholeness.

14. Each day, I honor the holistic nature of my existence, knowing that true healing encompasses all parts of who I am.

15. The holistic dance of healing brings fluidity to my life, each movement a step towards the realization of my complete self.

16. In the embrace of the tapestry of life, I find the threads of my past traumas gently woven into the strength of my present self.

17. My dedication to a holistic approach is a pledge to honor every facet of my being, fostering healing that is thorough and profound.

18. I am thankful for the holistic insights that guide me, offering clarity and unity as I heal from within.

19. Recognizing the mind-body-spirit connection, I nurture each part with equal devotion, for they all contribute to my story of resilience.

20. As I engage with the holistic dance of life, I am grateful for every twist and turn that teaches me more about the depth of my spirit and the potential for my healing.

CHAPTER 10

HOLISTIC VIEWPOINTS REDEFINED

We've all heard the saying, "The whole is greater than the sum of its parts." It's a profound thought that encapsulates the essence of the holistic approach. The term "holistic" often gets thrown around in wellness circles, sometimes ambiguously. But, when it comes to understanding trauma and its profound grip on us, holism offers a fresh, encompassing perspective.

The Holistic Landscape

Derived from the Greek word "holos," meaning "whole," holistic thinking urges us to see things in their entirety rather than isolated fragments (1). In terms of our well-being, this means recognizing the intricate interplay between our mind, body, and spirit, especially when navigating the mazes of trauma and healing.

Mind and Body: An Inseparable Duo

Often, we treat our mind and body as distinct entities. We go to the gym for our body, and perhaps, a therapist for our minds. But the two are deeply intertwined.

Imagine Anna, a woman in her thirties. As a child, she went through harrowing experiences of emotional abuse. On the surface, her trauma manifested as anxiety and recurrent nightmares. But dig a little deeper, and you'd find her often battling migraines and inexplicable fatigue. Her childhood trauma wasn't just a psychological scar; it reverberated through her body (2).

The Spirit: The Silent Anchor

While we regularly address the mind and body, the spirit often remains the unspoken component in many therapeutic realms. It's that ineffable essence that ties our experiences and perceptions together. When trauma strikes, it's not just our thoughts or physicality that get disrupted; our spirit, our core essence, feels the tremor too.

Reflect on Leo's story. He lost his parents in a tragic accident when he was only seven. While therapy helped him process the grief and the ensuing bouts of depression, there was an underlying spiritual disarray – a sense of purposelessness and detachment from life. It was only when he started attending group meditation sessions and spiritual workshops that Leo began to reconnect with his spirit, finding meaning and purpose (3).

Embracing Wholeness in Healing

So, why does this holistic approach matter? Because it offers a comprehensive path to healing. A fragmented approach might provide temporary relief, but for deep-rooted traumas, understanding the interconnection between mind, body, and spirit becomes paramount.

Let's consider a practical example. Yoga, which is now globally recognized, doesn't merely offer physical postures for body fitness. It combines breath (prana), postures (asanas), and mindfulness to provide healing at all levels – mental, physical, and spiritual (4).

Conclusion

Trauma, by its very nature, disrupts our wholeness. It fragments our perceptions and experiences, leaving us grappling with disparate pieces. The holistic approach, however, invites us to see the bigger picture, to understand the interwoven threads of our existence, and to heal in a manner that encompasses every facet of our being.

Through the holistic lens, we come to appreciate that true healing, especially from profound traumas, requires a comprehensive approach. By intertwining the mind, body, and spirit, we set the stage for deep, resonant healing that echoes through every facet of our existence.

References

1. Capra, F. (1996). *The Web of Life: A New Scientific Understanding of Living Systems.* Anchor Books.

2. Scaer, R. (2005). *The Trauma Spectrum: Hidden Wounds and Human Resiliency.* W.W. Norton & Company.

3. Koenig, H. G., King, D. E., & Carson, V. B. (2012). *Handbook of Religion and Health*. Oxford University Press.

4. Desikachar, T. K. V., Bragdon, E., & Bossart, C. (2005). *The Yoga of Healing: Exploring Yoga's Holistic Model for Health and Well-being*. International Journal of Yoga Therapy, 15(1), 17-39.

Chapter Ten Affirmations:

1. I redefine my view of healing, seeing it not as a linear process but as a holistic journey encompassing mind, body, and spirit.

2. In the holistic landscape of my inner world, every emotion, thought, and sensation has a place and purpose on my path to healing.

3. I affirm that my mind and body are inseparable allies in recovery, each informing and supporting the other.

4. My spirit, a silent anchor, holds me steady in turbulent seas, providing solace and strength as I navigate my healing.

5. Embracing wholeness, I recognize that every scar and smile, every memory and hope, are integral parts of my healing tapestry.

6. In the redefined holistic view, I find freedom; my trauma is not a life sentence but a chapter in my broader narrative of growth.

7. As I walk through the holistic landscape of recovery, I celebrate every step that brings me closer to harmony within myself.

8. I honor the unbreakable bond between my mind and body, cherishing their dialogue as the whispers of healing and self-discovery.

9. My spirit is the silent anchor, ever-present, ensuring that no storm can uproot my commitment to peace and self-acceptance.

10. Through wholeness, I heal, integrating every part of my being with gentle acceptance and profound gratitude.

11. I invite introspection, allowing it to illuminate the holistic viewpoints that redefine my relationship with my past.

12. In my holistic view, every experience is valuable, and I am thankful for the lessons that have shaped me.

13. Mind and body unite in their journey toward healing, a duo so powerful that no part of my trauma remains untouched by their care.

14. The spirit, often silent, is my unwavering source of hope and the bedrock of my inner peace.

15. I am whole, even in my healing; there is no part of me that is not worthy of love and acceptance.

16. Redefining healing, I find solace in the holistic approach that sees me, in my entirety, as a being capable of profound recovery.

17. Gratitude fills the holistic landscape of my mind, a serene garden where every thought is tended with care and compassion.

18. In the inseparable bond of mind and body, I find a healing force that moves me forward with unanticipated grace.

19. My spirit is the silent anchor, ensuring that self-acceptance is not just a concept, but a deeply felt reality.

20. Embracing my wholeness, I heal not just in parts, but as a complete, interconnected universe of potential, peace, and inner strength.

CHAPTER 11

THE POWER OF MINDFULNESS

I I Be here now." It's a simple phrase but carries profound wisdom. Mindfulness, a practice rooted in ancient Buddhist traditions, has taken the modern world by storm, finding its way into boardrooms, classrooms, therapy rooms, and even our living rooms. But why is mindfulness getting all this buzz, especially in the context of trauma recovery? Let's journey together into the serene world of mindfulness and its transformative effects on healing.

What is Mindfulness, Really?

At its essence, mindfulness is about being present, about grounding oneself in the current moment, irrespective of whether it's pleasant or painful (1). It's about observing without judgment, experiencing our thoughts, feelings, and sensations just as they are.

Mindfulness and Trauma: Why the Connection?

The mind, when faced with trauma, often operates in two modes: it either revisits the traumatic event, replaying it like a broken record or projects into the future, enveloped in fear and anxiety. What it forgets is the present moment.

Consider Emily, who survived a traumatic car accident. Every time she heard the screech of tires or a sudden horn, her heart raced, and she felt as if she were back in that harrowing moment. Or sometimes, she'd get anxious about future drives, even avoiding cars altogether. Her therapist introduced her to mindfulness meditation, where she learned to anchor herself in the present, observing her reactions without getting swept up in them (2).

The Science Behind It

It's not just anecdotal evidence that touts the benefits of mindfulness for trauma survivors. Neuroscientific research shows that mindfulness practice can bring about tangible changes in the brain regions associated with memory, emotion regulation, and self-awareness (3). Over time, consistent mindfulness practice can reduce the intensity of traumatic flashbacks and the accompanying physiological responses.

Tools and Techniques

So, how can one harness the power of mindfulness in trauma recovery? Here are some techniques:

1. **Mindful Breathing:** Simply focusing on one's breath can act as an anchor, drawing attention away from distressing thoughts and grounding the individual in the present (4).

2. **Body Scan Meditation:** This involves mentally scanning the body from head to toe, observing sensations without judgment. For trauma survivors, it can be a way to reconnect with their bodies.

3. **Mindful Walking:** A meditative walk, where one is fully aware of each step and the accompanying sensations, can be both grounding and therapeutic.

4. **Loving-kindness Meditation:** Sending out wishes of well-being to oneself and others can be particularly healing for individuals who've faced trauma, fostering feelings of compassion and reducing self-blame (5).

Mindfulness: Not a Panacea but a Powerful Ally

While mindfulness offers numerous benefits for trauma recovery, it's essential to approach it with an open heart and patience. Initially, diving deep into one's feelings and sensations might be overwhelming for some. It's always recommended to start slow, perhaps under the guidance of a trained professional.

Conclusion

The path of trauma recovery is neither linear nor predictable. But with tools like mindfulness, one can find pockets of peace, moments of respite, and gradually, a return to wholeness. By anchoring oneself in the present, one learns to observe the storms of trauma without getting swept away, making space for healing and growth.

Mindfulness, in its simplicity, offers a powerful respite from the turbulent waves of trauma. While it's not a 'magic pill', its consistent practice can pave the way for a deeper understanding of oneself and one's reactions, fostering resilience and promoting genuine healing.

References

1. Kabat-Zinn, J. (1994). *Wherever You Go, There You Are: Mindfulness Meditation in Everyday Life.* Hyperion.

2. van der Kolk, B. (2015). *The Body Keeps the Score: Brain, Mind, and Body in the Healing of Trauma.* Viking.

3. Holzel, B. K., Lazar, S. W., Gard, T., Schuman-Olivier, Z., Vago, D. R., & Ott, U. (2011). *How does mindfulness meditation work? Proposing mechanisms of action from a conceptual and neural perspective.* Perspectives on Psychological Science, 6(6), 537-559.

4. Germer, C. K., Siegel, R. D., & Fulton, P. R. (Eds.). (2016). *Mindfulness and psychotherapy (2nd ed.).* The Guilford Press.

5. Salzberg, S. (1995). *Lovingkindness: The Revolutionary Art of Happiness.* Shambhala Publications.

Chapter Eleven Affirmations:

1. Mindfulness is my sanctuary, a place of healing from childhood trauma, where each breath carries away a piece of my past's pain.

2. I embrace self-acceptance through mindfulness, acknowledging my journey and honoring my resilience.

3. In the quiet moments of mindfulness, I find inner peace, a calm center in the midst of life's storms.

4. Gratitude blooms as I practice mindfulness, recognizing the beauty of the present and the strength I've garnered from my past.

5. Through introspection, mindfulness allows me to explore the depths of my soul and spirit, finding treasures amidst the trials.

6. I ask, "What is mindfulness, really?" and discover it's a gentle, steadfast companion on my journey to healing.

7. In connecting mindfulness and trauma, I uncover why they align – for in this mindful space, healing finds fertile ground.

8. The science behind mindfulness reassures me; this is a path well-trodden with evidence of peace and recovery.

9. With each mindful tool and technique, I build a fortress of serenity around me, a defense against old wounds.

10. Mindfulness teaches me to inhabit the present, acknowledging pain without letting it define me.

11. Each mindful moment is not an escape but an acceptance, a powerful ally in recognizing my trauma without letting it hold sway.

12. I use mindfulness to gently navigate through memories, knowing that with this compass, I won't lose my way.

13. Mindfulness is not my panacea, but it is a powerful ally, a way to steady my heart when the echoes of trauma whisper.

14. With mindfulness, I learn the true meaning of healing: it's not about erasing the past but transforming my relationship with it.

15. Through mindfulness, I gain a deeper understanding of my responses to trauma and learn new, compassionate ways to address them.

16. Each technique of mindfulness I practice is a step towards a future where trauma does not hold the reins of my soul or spirit.

17. I find solace in the science that backs mindfulness, knowing that my healing is grounded in both spiritual and empirical truth.

18. In the practice of mindfulness, I find a balance, understanding it's not a cure but a method to live more fully, even with my history.

19. With every mindful breath, I affirm my commitment to the journey, not just to survive my past but to thrive despite it.

20. Mindfulness brings me back to a state of gratitude, for it's in the present that I can shape a new and compassionate narrative for my life.

CHAPTER 12

INTEGRATIVE HEALING

"Two hands are better than one," goes the old saying. But when it comes to healing from trauma, it might be apt to say, "Multiple approaches are better than one." Integrative healing is like the proverbial mixing of the East and West, combining time-tested traditional practices with holistic alternative therapies. Let's embark on a pilgrimage together into this blended world, where old meets new, and science intersects with soul.

Why Go Integrative?

In traditional medicine, say you're presented with a pill or a particular treatment for an ailment, and that's mostly where it ends. But trauma, especially childhood trauma, is a complicated web that affects the mind, body, and soul (1). This calls for a more comprehensive approach, doesn't it?

Let's take a quick example. Imagine someone—let's call him James, who has faced consistent neglect in his childhood. He grows up with a chronic sense of worthlessness, leading to depression. While anti-depressants might help him manage his symptoms, exploring art therapy might allow him to express his suppressed feelings. Furthermore, acupuncture might help balance the energy disrupted by prolonged emotional distress.

The Best of Both Worlds

1. **Talk Therapies and Psychotherapy:** Traditionally, this is the cornerstone of addressing trauma. Techniques such as cognitive-behavioral therapy (CBT) or dialectical behavior therapy (DBT) help reshape harmful thought patterns (2)

2. **Body-based Therapies:** Modalities like yoga, tai chi, or qigong emphasize the mind-body connection, fostering physical healing that complements emotional well-being (3).

3. **Energy Healing:** Reiki, acupuncture, and pranic healing are practices rooted in the belief that the body has energy centers. Balancing this energy can often lead to emotional and physical healing (4).

4. **Expressive Arts Therapy:** Painting, music, dance, or drama aren't just for fun. They can be therapeutic tools that allow individuals to express and process their emotions (5).

5. **Nature Therapy:** A walk in the park or a hike isn't just recreational. The great outdoors has a calming effect on the human psyche, grounding us and providing respite from chaotic thoughts.

A Tailored Approach

The beauty of integrative healing is its flexibility. Not every modality will resonate with everyone, and that's okay. The aim is to find the right combination that addresses the unique needs of the individual.

For instance, Lucy, a survivor of childhood bullying, might find solace in talk therapy but also feel empowered through kickboxing classes. Mark, who lost a parent early on, might benefit from group therapy and forest healing walks (6)

Navigating Integrative Healing

Choosing to walk the path of integrative healing demands open-mindedness and a pinch of curiosity. It's about collaboration between the individual and the therapist, constantly adjusting and realigning based on what works best.

Conclusion

Integrative healing paints a future of trauma recovery that's not about choosing between the old and the new but harmoniously merging them for the individual's highest good. It acknowledges that we're not just a sum of our parts, but a dynamic interplay of mind, body, and spirit.

The journey of healing is personal and unique. While there's no one-size-fits-all, an integrative approach ensures that every individual has a vast toolbox to dive into, picking and choosing what resonates, and weaving a healing narrative that's exclusively their own.

References

1. Siegel, D. J. (2010). *The Mindful Therapist: A Clinician's Guide to Mindsight and Neural Integration.* W. W. Norton & Company.

2. Linehan, M. M. (2014). *DBT Skills Training Manual (2nd ed.).* The Guilford Press.

3. McCall, T. (2007). *Yoga as Medicine: The Yogic Prescription for Health and Healing.* Bantam.

4. Rand, W. (2000). *Reiki: The Healing Touch - First and Second Degree Manual.* Vision Publications.

5. Malchiodi, C. A. (2005). *Expressive Therapies.* The Guilford Press.

6. Jordan, M., & Hinds, J. (Eds.). (2016). *Ecotherapy: Theory, Research and Practice.* Macmillan International Higher Education.

Chapter Twelve Affirmations

1. I embrace integrative healing, uniting the wisdom of ancient and modern to mend the wounds of childhood trauma.

2. In the fusion of therapies, I find the unique alchemy for my healing – a path paved with self-acceptance and care.

3. Integrative healing brings me inner peace, as it acknowledges the complexity of my experiences with a holistic embrace.

4. I am grateful for the convergence of diverse healing practices that honor both my vulnerability and my strength.

5. Through introspection, integrative healing allows me to explore the multifaceted nature of my soul and spirit.

6. "Why go integrative?" I ask, and my heart answers: to weave a tapestry of recovery rich with color and texture.

7. In this journey, I discover the best of both worlds: the precision of science and the wisdom of tradition.

8. Each step in my tailored approach to healing is chosen with intention, tailored to my unique narrative and needs.

9. Navigating integrative healing, I become the cartographer of my wellbeing, mapping a route to wholeness.

10. Integrative healing respects my individuality, blending practices to fit the contours of my personal story of resilience.

11. With integrative healing, I build a mosaic of therapies, each piece a testament to my commitment to healing.

12. In this journey, every modality offers a different lens, bringing my inner landscape into clearer view.

13. The integrative path teaches me gratitude for every element in my healing process, each a vital strand in the web of recovery.

14. As I weave conventional and alternative therapies into my healing, I find a balance that resonates with my deepest self.

15. Integrative healing is not just a method, but a dialogue between my past, present, and the peace I'm cultivating.

16. This blend of healing practices becomes a chorus, each voice singing a note of harmony, self-love, and acceptance.

17. The question of "Why go integrative?" is answered in each moment of synergy, where combined therapies echo my desire to heal wholly.

18. The best of both worlds in healing brings a symphony of resources to my doorstep, inviting me to dance to the rhythm of recovery.

19. A tailored approach means I am seen, I am heard, and my healing is as unique as the tapestry of my life experiences.

20. Navigating integrative healing, I honor the complexity of my trauma with a rich complexity of healing, embracing every lesson and gift on this path.

CHAPTER 13

NATURE'S BALM

| | Look deep into nature, and then you will understand everything better," mused Albert Einstein. Indeed, our connection with nature is intrinsic, primal, and often overlooked in our busy, tech-saturated lives. However, if we were to stop, breathe, and simply 'be' in nature, the healing effects on a trauma-ridden soul can be profoundly transformative. So, let's step into the great outdoors and explore the eco-therapeutic power of nature in trauma recovery.

Nature as a Therapist

Picture this:

- Walking through a dense forest.
- Listening to the harmonious chirping of birds.
- Feeling the soft moss beneath your feet.
- Letting the scent of fresh pine envelop you.

Sounds tranquil, right? That's the heart of ecotherapy (1). It's not just about being in nature; it's about *connecting* with nature.

Many of us remember playing outside as children, building forts, climbing trees, and generally having a ball. In these moments, we were present, grounded, and free from the burdens of life. It's that exact child-like wonder and engagement that nature therapy taps into.

Science Behind the Serenity

It's not all poetic. Science backs it up too! Nature has shown to reduce cortisol levels, the stress hormone, thereby alleviating anxiety (2). The phenomenon of "forest bathing" in Japan, known as Shinrin-Yoku, underscores the idea that immersing oneself in a forest setting can boost mood, lower anxiety, reduce stress, and even improve sleep (3).

Furthermore, the act of grounding, or walking barefoot on natural surfaces, is believed to neutralize negative ions in our bodies, promoting physical well-being and emotional tranquility (4).

Real-World Instances: Nature's Miracles

Emma's Story: Emma grew up in a tumultuous household. As an escape, she would often wander into the woods behind her home. It was her sanctuary. As an adult grappling with anxiety, she found solace returning to those woods, learning to meditate by the serene brooks, and practicing mindful walking. Nature was her healer, the constant amid chaos.

Urban Healing Gardens: City dwellers often feel the absence of green spaces acutely. Recognizing this, many urban environments are now creating healing gardens — spaces designed to provide sensory engagement, relaxation, and solace5. These gardens become sanctuaries in the concrete jungle, helping many navigate their urban lives with a touch of nature's tranquility.

Making Nature Therapy Accessible

While strolling through woods or taking forest baths sounds dreamy, it might not be accessible for everyone. But that's okay. Nature therapy can be as simple as tending to a plant at home, visiting a local park, or even just listening to nature sounds. The key is intentionality, immersion, and connection.

Herbal Remedies: Nature's Apothecary

For centuries, cultures around the world have turned to the earth's bounty for healing — finding potent remedies in herbs. Herbs such as turmeric, renowned for its anti-inflammatory properties due to its curcumin content, and ginger, which has been used to aid digestion and alleviate nausea, stand out for their medicinal benefits. The active compounds found in these plants, such as antioxidants, can neutralize free radicals and reduce oxidative stress, which is implicated in a multitude of chronic diseases.

Moreover, adaptogenic herbs like ashwagandha and rhodiola can help the body manage stress more effectively, offering a buffer against the toll of modern life's pressures. Scientific research continues to support these uses, showing that herbal medicine, when used correctly, can be a powerful tool for maintaining health and treating disease (5).

Spices: The Flavor of Wellness

Spices do more than just enhance the flavor of food — they can also contribute to better health. Cinnamon, for instance, is believed to have blood sugar-lowering properties, making it a topic of interest for diabetes research. Capsaicin, the compound that gives chili peppers their heat, is used in topical ointments for its pain-relieving properties. Furthermore, spices like cloves and cardamom contain compounds that have been studied for their antimicrobial and anti-inflammatory effects (6). These culinary treasures offer a double benefit: they can make food more enjoyable while simultaneously supporting bodily functions and overall wellness.

Minerals and Vitamins: Microscopic Architects of Health

Minerals and vitamins are essential micronutrients that act as the microscopic architects of our health. Calcium and magnesium are vital for bone health, while iron is crucial for transporting oxygen throughout the body. Vitamins like Vitamin D, obtained from sunlight or fortified foods, is pivotal for calcium absorption and bone health, and

Vitamin C is essential for the repair of body tissues and the efficient functioning of the immune system. B vitamins play a critical role in energy metabolism and brain health. The delicate balance of these micronutrients is crucial; even a minor deficiency can have significant impacts on health, reinforcing the importance of a varied and nutrient-rich diet (7).

High-Vibration Foods: Eating for Energetic Harmony

The concept of high-vibration foods is rooted in the belief that foods carry vibrational energy that can impact our own energy fields. Fresh, organic produce and whole foods are considered high in vibrational frequency and are said to enhance one's vitality and well-being. Advocates of this approach argue that consuming these foods can lead to clearer thinking, more energy, and a deeper sense of connection to the environment. While empirical evidence on the vibrational qualities of food is limited, the health benefits of consuming a diet rich in fruits, vegetables, whole grains, and lean proteins are well-documented, aligning with recommendations for preventing chronic diseases and supporting overall health (8).

Psychedelic Plant Medicine: An Ancient Future Therapy

Psychedelics, when mentioned in the context of plant medicine, refer to substances like psilocybin, found in magic mushrooms, or ayahuasca, a brew made from Amazonian plants. Indigenous cultures have used these substances for spiritual and medicinal purposes for millennia. In a controlled and safe environment, under professional guidance, modern therapeutic use of psychedelics is being explored for its potential to treat a variety of mental health issues, such as depression, PTSD, and addiction. Research is showing promising results, with many participants reporting profound experiences leading to long-lasting positive changes in their mental health (9).

Nature as a Co-journeyer in Healing

In trauma recovery, nature doesn't play the role of a distant healer but rather a companion. It doesn't offer quick fixes but instead provides a space for introspection, growth, and understanding.

Conclusion

In our journey of healing and self-discovery, nature emerges not just as a backdrop but an active participant. It listens without judgment, cradles without conditions, and heals without expectations. As we navigate the tumultuous waters of trauma recovery, nature stands by our side as a timeless balm, offering solace and serenity.

In the tapestry of healing, nature weaves its magic thread, mending the frayed edges of our souls and leading us to a place of peace and understanding.

References

1. Jordan, M., & Hinds, J. (Eds.). (2016). *Ecotherapy: Theory, Research and Practice.* Macmillan International Higher Education.

2. Bratman, G. N., Daily, G. C., Levy, B. J., & Gross, J. J. (2015). The benefits of nature experience: Improved affect and cognition. *Landscape and Urban Planning, 138,* 41-50.

3. Park, B. J., Tsunetsugu, Y., Kasetani, T., Kagawa, T., & Miyazaki, Y. (2010). The physiological effects of Shinrin-yoku (taking in the forest atmosphere or forest bathing): evidence from field experiments in 24 forests across Japan. *Environmental health and preventive medicine, 15*(1), 18-26.

4. Oschman, J. L., Chevalier, G., & Brown, R. (2015). The effects of grounding (earthing) on inflammation, the immune response, wound healing, and prevention and treatment of chronic inflammatory and autoimmune diseases. *Journal of Inflammation Research, 8,* 83.

5. Marcus, C. C., & Sachs, N. A. (2014). *Therapeutic landscapes: An evidence-based approach to designing healing gardens and restorative outdoor spaces.* John Wiley & Sons.

6. Chevallier, A. (2016). *Encyclopedia of Herbal Medicine.* DK Publishing.

7.   Aggarwal, B. B., & Kunnumakkara, A. B. (2017). *Molecular Targets and Therapeutic Uses of Spices: Modern Uses for Ancient Medicine*. World Scientific Publishing Co.

8.   Haas, E. M., & Levin, B. (2018). *Staying Healthy with Nutrition*. Celestial Arts. Pollan, M. (2008). *In Defense of Food: An Eater's Manifesto*. Penguin Books.

9.   Griffiths, R. R., Johnson, M. W., Carducci, M. A., Umbricht, A., Richards, W. A., Richards, B. D., ... & Klinedinst, M. A. (2016). Psilocybin produces substantial and sustained decreases in depression and anxiety in patients with life-threatening cancer: A randomized double-blind trial. *Journal of Psychopharmacology*, 30(12), 1181-1197.

Chapter Thirteen Affirmations:

1. I acknowledge nature as my therapist, its tranquil presence a balm for the wounds of childhood trauma.

2. In every rustle of leaves and whisper of the wind, I find the serenity that science acknowledges as healing.

3. I embrace the healing power of nature, making its therapy accessible in daily walks, gardening, and moments under the sky.

4. With gratitude, I turn to nature's apothecary, finding remedies in the hues of flowers and the scents of herbs.

5. I savor spices, not only as the flavor of wellness but as nature's gentle healers, infusing my meals with healing properties.

6. I nourish my body with minerals and vitamins, the microscopic architects that rebuild me from within.

7. In high-vibration foods, I find energetic harmony, a gift from nature to align my body and soul.

8. I explore the ancient wisdom of plant medicine with respect, recognizing its potential in guided, mindful healing.

9. Nature accompanies me on my healing journey, a co-journeyer whose silent wisdom speaks directly to my spirit.

10. I am open to the teachings of the natural world, allowing its subtle yet profound messages to guide my introspection.

11. I accept the healing embrace of nature, finding a deep connection that fosters self-acceptance and growth.

12. I am grateful for the symphony of life surrounding me, a natural orchestra that plays the soundtrack of recovery.

13. Every element of nature I encounter mirrors a part of my healing, teaching me lessons of resilience and transformation.

14. I engage with nature mindfully, allowing its rhythm to teach me the art of inner peace and presence.

15. As I walk through natural landscapes, I am reminded of my own inner landscape, ripe with the potential for healing and peace.

16. I trust in the science behind nature's serenity, allowing it to fortify my journey toward healing childhood trauma.

17. Nature's accessibility reminds me that healing is always within reach in the sunlight, the earth, and the air I breathe.

18. Through nature's apothecary, I find a treasure trove of natural remedies that enhance my well-being and vitality.

19. I honor the spices, minerals, and foods that come from the earth, each one an affirmation of life's vibrant potential for healing.

20. As nature's co-journeyer, I tread a path of recovery interwoven with green leaves and blue skies, an ever-present testament to the resilience sown in both nature and myself.

CHAPTER 14
THE PATH TO RESILIENCE

Out of suffering have emerged the strongest souls; the most massive characters are seared with scars," wrote Khalil Gibran. Resilience is a quality not magically imparted but forged in the fires of adversity. But, how do some people rise from the ashes of their traumas while others remain entrenched in their pain? The answer, quite beautifully, lies in the realms of self-compassion, forgiveness, and acceptance. Let's unpack this incredible journey together.

Understanding Resilience: It's Not Just "Bouncing Back"

Before diving deep, let's bust a myth: resilience isn't just about "bouncing back" to who you were before the trauma. It's about growing, evolving, and becoming even stronger, like a phoenix rising from the ashes (1). It's about post-traumatic growth.

Self-compassion: Holding Your Own Hand

We're often our harshest critics, aren't we? Especially when faced with trauma, we might berate ourselves with thoughts like, "Why can't I just get over it?" or "Others have it worse." This is where self-compassion steps in.

Self-compassion is about treating ourselves with the same kindness, concern, and understanding that we would offer to a dear friend (2).

Real-world Insight: Meet Daniel. After a childhood filled with neglect, he was prone to beating himself up over minor mistakes. Once he learned about self-compassion through therapy, he started a nightly ritual. Each night, he would journal three instances where he showed himself compassion that day. Over time, this practice transformed his self-view.

Forgiveness: Unshackling the Soul

Ah, forgiveness. It sounds simple but is often a mountainous task, especially when the harm was serious. But here's the twist: forgiveness is less about the perpetrator and more about the victim. It's about letting go of grudges, resentment, and thoughts of revenge — for one's own peace (3).

Real-world Insight: Lila witnessed a heinous crime in her teens. For years, she harbored anger and fantasies of revenge. Attending a support group, she realized forgiveness was her path to healing. Slowly, through introspection and therapy, she learned to forgive, not for the offender's sake, but to free her own soul.

Acceptance: Embracing the New You

The trauma might change us. And that's okay. Acceptance is about understanding that it's okay to be different post-trauma and allowing oneself to grieve the losses while also embracing the growth (4).

Real-world Insight: After a car accident, Jake struggled with mobility issues. He mourned his days of running marathons. Through therapy, he learned the art of acceptance. He found new hobbies, like painting and writing, and realized that while one chapter had closed, another had beautifully begun.

Building Blocks of Resilience: Practical Strategies

1. **Educate Yourself:** Understand trauma and its effects. The more you know, the less you'll blame yourself.

2. **Social Support:** Join support groups, lean on friends and family, or consider professional help.

3. **Physical Wellness:** Activities like yoga or even a simple walk can be incredibly grounding (5).

4. **Mindfulness Practices:** Techniques like meditation or deep breathing can center the soul.

5. **Journaling:** Writing can offer a safe space to confront and process feelings.

Conclusion

Trauma might be a chapter, or even several chapters, in the book of our lives, but it isn't the whole story. With self-compassion, forgiveness, and acceptance as our guides, we can write our narrative of resilience and growth. As the Japanese proverb goes, "Nanakorobi yaoki" – fall down seven times, get up eight.

In the end, resilience is a journey, not a destination. With each step forward, we are writing our own story of triumph and hope.

References

1. Southwick, S. M., Bonanno, G. A., Masten, A. S., Panter-Brick, C., & Yehuda, R. (2014). Resilience definitions, theory, and challenges: interdisciplinary perspectives. *European journal of psychotraumatology*, 5(1), 25338.

2. Neff, K. (2011). *Self-compassion, self-esteem, and well-being.* Social and Personality Psychology Compass, 5(1), 1-12.

3. Enright, R. D., & Fitzgibbons, R. P. (2015). *Forgiveness therapy: An empirical guide for resolving anger and restoring hope.* American Psychological Association.

4. Hayes, S. C., Strosahl, K. D., & Wilson, K. G. (1999). *Acceptance and Commitment Therapy.* American Psychological Association.

5. Van der Kolk, B. (2015). *The body keeps the score: Brain, mind, and body in the healing of trauma.* Penguin Books.

Chapter Fourteen Affirmations:

1. I understand resilience as a journey, not merely a rebound, but a renaissance of the soul that has weathered storms.

2. In my path to resilience, I recognize my strength, which is sculpted by the tides of past traumas and present healing.

3. I hold my hand with compassion, nurturing my inner child with kindness and care through each step towards resilience.

4. With self-compassion, I create a sanctuary within, where healing is the air I breathe, and self-acceptance is the ground I walk on.

5. I practice forgiveness, knowing it frees my soul from the chains of the past, allowing me to move forward with grace.

6. Forgiveness is my proclamation of peace to myself; it's my declaration of independence from the pain that once held me captive.

7. I embrace acceptance, knowing it is the vessel that carries me toward new horizons, new dreams, and the new me.

8. Acceptance is not surrender; it is the wisdom to inhabit the present fully and shape the future with intention.

9.   I am building my resilience daily, with each act of self-care, each boundary set, and each moment of mindfulness.

10. Practical strategies like journaling, affirmations, and therapy are the bricks that lay the foundation of my resilience.

11. I celebrate every small victory on my path, for they are the threads that weave the tapestry of my resilient spirit.

12. In understanding resilience, I find the courage to be vulnerable and the strength to rise again, wiser and more grounded.

13. Self-compassion whispers to me during tough times, reminding me that I am enough and that my journey matters.

14. Each act of forgiveness is a step towards a future unburdened by resentment, where my spirit can soar freely.

15. I embody the new me, an alchemy of past lessons and future aspirations, an ever-evolving masterpiece of resilience.

16. Gratitude infuses my path to resilience, for each challenge overcome is a testament to my strength and growth.

17. Inner peace is the reward of my resilience, a serene acceptance of my past, and a hopeful embrace of what lies ahead.

18. Through introspection, I discover the bedrock of my resilience, forged in the fire of my experiences and quenched in the waters of healing.

19. My soul and spirit are partners in this dance of resilience, moving in harmony with the rhythm of life's continuous unfolding.

20. The path to resilience is uniquely mine, a sacred journey of returning home to the deepest, most authentic part of myself.

CONCLUSION: THE SYMPHONY OF HEALING

As we reach the end of this exploration into childhood trauma and the multifaceted paths toward healing, it's essential to recognize the strength and resilience that exists within each individual. We have journeyed through the various traumas and their profound effects on the mind, body, and soul, and we have delved into the holistic and integrative techniques that can pave the way to recovery. The journey may be challenging, but with understanding, support, and persistence, it is one filled with hope and transformation.

Throughout this book, after every chapter, we incorporated affirmations. Now, why did we do that?

Affirmations are short, powerful statements that, when repeated often, can change the way we think and feel. As Dr. Candace Pert highlighted in her groundbreaking work, our thoughts can influence our bodies at the molecular level (1). For survivors of childhood trauma, negative self-talk, guilt, shame, and feelings of unworthiness can become deeply ingrained. Such individuals might even unknowingly replay harmful narratives, thus perpetuating a cycle of pain and self-sabotage.

This is where affirmations come into play. By consciously choosing and repeating positive statements, we can start reprogramming our subconscious mind (2). Over time, these affirmations can counteract the effects of negative self-talk, replace limiting beliefs, and promote healing. They serve as gentle reminders of one's worth, strength, and capacity for growth.

Real-world Insight: Consider Jane, a survivor of childhood neglect. Growing up, the constant refrain in her mind was, "I am not worthy of love." Through therapy and self-help, Jane started using the affirmation, "I am deserving of unconditional love and acceptance." Over time, this simple statement began to chip away at her deeply held negative beliefs, opening her heart to love and healing.

For many survivors of childhood trauma, the journey towards healing isn't linear. There might be setbacks along the way. But with tools like affirmations, coupled with therapy and holistic approaches, individuals can progressively reclaim their narrative. They can transcend their trauma, not as damaged individuals but as resilient warriors with stories of incredible strength and growth.

In the words of Rumi, "The wound is the place where the light enters you." Let's remember this profound wisdom by embracing our wounds and allowing the light of healing to illuminate our path forward.

To all the readers, survivors, and supporters alike, remember that each day is a step toward healing. Embrace the journey, lean on the resources available, and always,

always believe in the transformative power of the human spirits.

Remember, with each affirmation, we're not just saying words; we're building bridges to a brighter, healed self. Keep walking, keep affirming, and keep healing.

References

1. Pert, C. (1999). *Molecules of Emotion: The Science Behind Mind-Body Medicine.* Simon and Schuster.

2. Dispenza, J. (2012). *Breaking the Habit of Being Yourself: How to Lose Your Mind and Create a New One.* Hay House.

AUTHOR'S REFLECTION

When I embarked on this journey of exploring and writing about childhood traumas, their profound impacts, and the paths toward healing, I was driven by a deep curiosity and an unwavering belief in the human spirit's resilience. While I anticipated learning and sharing academic knowledge, I hadn't fully prepared for the personal transformation this process would induce.

Every chapter penned and every survivor's story I delved into left an indelible mark on my psyche. The sheer magnitude of pain and suffering endured by so many became palpably real. But even more striking was the resilient spirit that many showcased, the unyielding will to not just survive but thrive. Their stories were not just of pain but also of hope, courage, and transformation.

I've come to realize that trauma, while devastating, doesn't define a person. Instead, it's their response to it, their journey of healing, and their rediscovered sense of purpose that truly shapes their essence. This book, in many ways, is a testament to that belief.

As I penned down holistic approaches and healing modalities, a profound truth became evident: Healing is as multifaceted as the traumas themselves. There isn't a one-size-fits-all solution. However, the interconnection of mind, body, and spirit remains a universal thread. Recognizing this interplay, respecting it, and leveraging it forms the crux of holistic healing.

Including affirmations after each chapter became a personal ritual. As someone who has dabbled with affirmations in my personal life, I've always been intrigued by their transformative power. Through this book, they acted as gentle reminders for me, and hopefully for the readers, about the innate strength each one of us holds.

A recurring theme in many conversations and interviews conducted during the research phase was the power of sharing one's story. Narrating one's experiences — the lows and the highs, the pains and the triumphs — seemed therapeutic for many. It drove home the fact that healing is also about community, about finding and giving support, and about collective growth.

In conclusion, this book, while aimed at educating and aiding, has been deeply personal. It's a journey I've taken alongside every reader, every survivor, every therapist, and every healer. The lessons learned, the stories shared, and the hope rekindled will forever remain etched in my heart.

To every individual who finds solace, guidance, or even a mere acknowledgment of their experiences in these pages, I extend my deepest gratitude. Your journey inspires mine. And to every soul still seeking answers and healing, remember, the journey may be long, but the destination is worth every step.

With gratitude and hope,

Mel

Forgiveness:

1. I acknowledge my past and forgive myself for holding onto it.

2. My forgiveness is a gift I give to myself, a release from pain.

3. With each passing moment, I'm choosing the path of forgiveness and healing.

4. My heart is expansive, and within it, there's room for understanding and forgiveness.

5. I release all anger and bitterness as I wholeheartedly embrace the power of forgiveness.

6. By forgiving, I'm not forgetting; I'm allowing my soul to find peace.

7. I deserve the tranquility and liberation that comes with forgiveness.

8. Every day I'm learning to forgive those who hurt me, and in doing so, I'm setting myself free.

9. I am breaking the chains of the past with the strength of my forgiveness.

10. I know that forgiveness is a journey, and I'm patient with my progress.

11. By forgiving, I'm evolving, growing, and maturing.

12. I understand that forgiveness is a sign of strength, not weakness.

13. As I tread the path of healing, I'm empowered by my own forgiveness.

14. My forgiveness is the first step towards a brighter, more hopeful future.

15. I am in control of my narrative, and I choose forgiveness as my ally.

Self-Love:

1. I deeply and unconditionally love and accept myself.

2. Every fiber of my being radiates self-love and acceptance.

3. I recognize my worth and treat myself with kindness and love.

4. Each day, my love for myself grows stronger and more profound.

5. I cherish who I am, with all my strengths and imperfections.

6. Loving myself is the foundation of my inner strength and happiness.

7. I am deserving of the same love that I give to others.

8. By loving myself, I attract positive energy and abundance into my life.

9. My self-love empowers and rejuvenates me in every situation.

10. I prioritize my well-being and happiness because I truly love myself.

11. My journey towards healing is fueled by relentless self-love.

12. Loving myself is an act of courage and strength.

13. Through the lens of self-love, I see my true potential.

14. My self-love is the compass that guides me through life.

15. I am a reflection of love, and I shine brightly.

Self-Esteem:

1. I believe in my capabilities and recognize my unique worth.

2. My self-worth is independent of others' opinions or validations.

3. Every challenge I face reinforces my self-esteem and resilience.

4. I am proud of my achievements and embrace my failures as lessons.

5. My self-esteem is the armor that shields me from negativity.

6. I radiate confidence and positivity.

7. I deserve all the good that comes my way, and I claim it with pride.

8. My self-esteem is grounded in reality, and I see myself for who I truly am.

9. I am deserving of respect, love, and kindness.

10. My confidence is a beacon that guides others and inspires them.

11. I celebrate my uniqueness and everything that makes me, me.

12. By honoring myself, I uplift my self-esteem.

13. Every compliment I receive is a reflection of my true essence.

14. My journey, with its ups and downs, amplifies my self-worth.

15. My self-esteem is unwavering, for I am grounded in my truth.

Grace:

1. I navigate life's challenges with grace and poise.

2. My presence radiates grace, drawing others towards me.

3. Even in adversity, I remain graceful, understanding, and calm.

4. I handle every situation with grace, reflecting my inner strength.

5. Grace is my silent power, evident in my actions and words.

6. Every step I take is infused with elegance and grace.

7. My spirit exudes grace, lighting up every room I enter.

8. By embracing grace, I elevate my experiences and relationships.

9. My grace is a testament to my journey and growth.

10. In moments of doubt, I lean into grace for clarity.

11. Through grace, I find harmony in chaos.

12. My grace is my shield, protecting and uplifting me.

13. Grace allows me to see beauty in every situation.

14. I am the epitome of grace, resilience, and strength.

15. With grace, I transcend challenges and soar to new heights.

Compassion:

1. My heart overflows with compassion for myself and others.

2. Compassion is the bridge that connects me to the world.

3. I approach every situation with a heart full of understanding and compassion.

4. By showing compassion, I heal not just others but also myself.

5. Compassion is my guiding light, illuminating the path of love.

6. In moments of pain, I find solace in my own compassion.

7. My compassion has the power to transform pain into purpose.

8. I recognize the strength in showing compassion even when it's tough.

9. Through compassion, I see the world through a lens of love.

10. My compassion is a reflection of my deep understanding of human nature.

11. By embracing compassion, I enrich my soul and the souls of others.

12. Compassion is the thread that weaves together the tapestry of humanity.

13. My compassionate nature is a gift, and I share it generously.

14. Every act of kindness stems from my deep reservoir of compassion.

15. In a world that can be harsh, my compassion is a beacon of hope.

Gratitude:

1. My heart is a wellspring of gratitude for all that I have and all that I am.

2. Every day, I count my blessings and express gratitude for life's abundance.

3. Gratitude is the key that unlocks the door to happiness and contentment.

4. I cherish every moment, for it's a gift I'm deeply grateful for.

5. Through gratitude, I transform ordinary moments into extraordinary memories.

6. My gratitude amplifies the beauty in my life.

7. I express gratitude for the lessons learned, even in challenging times.

8. With a grateful heart, I attract positivity and blessings.

9. My gratitude is a magnet for miracles.

10. By practicing gratitude daily, I enrich my soul and perspective.

11. Gratitude reminds me of the interconnectedness of all things.

12. I am deeply thankful for the love, support.

For more information about this author and for speaking engagement, visit www.harmelcodijd.com or email harmelcodijd@gmail.com

More books from this author, visit www.teachmehowbooks.com

Made in the USA
Columbia, SC
21 January 2024

29812549R00076